ROYAL COURT

Short Course.
April – June 05

Royal Court Theatre presents

BONE

by John Donnelly

First performance at the Royal Court Jerwood Theatre Upstairs, Sloane Square, London
on 9 September 2004.

BONE is presented as part of the YOUNG PLAYWRIGHTS' SEASON 2004, a Genesis Project.

ONE

John Donnelly

st in order of appearance

len **Brid Brennan**

phen **Don Gilet**

nie **Bryan Dick**

rector **Femi Elufowoju, jr**

signer **Ultz**

hting Designers **Ultz, Trevor Wallace**

und Designer **Emma Laxton**

sistant Director **Lucy Kerbel**

sting **Amy Ball**

oduction Manager **Sue Bird**

ge Management **Sally Higson, Dani Youngman**

stume Supervisors **Iona Kenrick, Jackie Orton**

mpany Voice Work **Patsy Rodenburg**

John Donnelly (writer)

For the Royal Court: There (Rampage Festival – Young Writers Programme).

Other theatre includes: Finally the Girl (Old Red Lion); Five Songs of Grace and Redemption (Liminal Theatre); Hack! (Jermyn Street Theatre); Hope to Die (St Martin's, Melbourne); Slave/Teacher (Lyric); Personal Matters (BAC); Sex and Death (Edinburgh Festival Fringe).

As an actor: Tartuffe, Thyestes (Edinburgh Festival Fringe); The Wheel (Munich Film School/NSFTV).

Awards include: 1997 NSDF Sunday Times Playwriting Award for Sex and Death, PMA Writer/Director Award and a Three Weeks New Works Award for the ten best new plays at the Edinburgh Festival Fringe.

Brid Brennan

For the Royal Court: Bailegangaire, Up to the Sun and Down to the Centre, Ourselves Alone.

Other theatre includes: The Dark, Little Foxes, A Kind of Alaska (Donmar); Absolutely! (Perhaps) (Wyndham's); 10 Rounds (Tricycle); A Kind of Alaska (Lincoln Center Pinter Festival, New York); Juno and the Paycock (Gaiety, Dublin); Macbeth, La Lupa (RSC); Dancing at Lughnasa, Rutherford and Son, Machine Wreckers, Man Beast and Virtue (NT); Dancing at Lughnasa (West End/Abbey, Dublin/Plymouth, Broadway); Smelling a Rat (Hampstead); Holy Days (Soho); Perdition (Conway Hall); The Shaugraun, The Playboy of the Western World (Druid Theatre Company); Edward II (Royal Exchange, Manchester); Gold in the Streets (Boston Shakespeare Company).

Television includes: Anytime Now, Hidden City, Sunday, Cracker 11, Hedda Gabler, Tell Tale Heart, Ghostwatch, Itch, The Birmingham Six, South of the Border, Upline, Four Days in July, The Ballroom of Romance, The Daily Woman, Too Late to Talk to Billy, A Matter of Choice for Billy, A Coming of Terms for Billy, Lorna, Bracken.

Film includes: Sunday, Topsy Turvy, Felicia's Journey, Dancing at Lughnasa, Trojan Eddie, St. Ex, Words upon a Window Pane, Anne Devlin, Maeve, Ursula and Glenys, Hidden City, She's Been Away, Excalibur.

Radio includes: His Dark Materials, Twinkle Toes and Yerma (BBC).

Awards include: Irish Academy Award Winner for Best Actress in Dancing at Lughnasa, 1999; Tony Award for Best Supporting Actress for Dancing at Lughnasa, 1992.

Bryan Dick

For the Royal Court: Sliding with Suzanne, Plasticine.

Other theatre includes: School Play (Soho

Television includes: Blackpool, The Long F Passer By, Bed Time, White Teeth, Clocking Off – Series 2, North Square, Foyle's War, Shockers: Parents' Night, Red Cap – Series 2, Bunk Bed Boys, Blue Murder, Strange, The Life and Times Henry Pratt, Speaking in Tongues, Bonjour Classe, Earthfasts, Dalziel and Pascoe, The Bill, Mersey Beat.

Film includes: Master and Commander, Morvern Callar, Colour Me Kubrick, Drea

Femi Elufowoju, jr (director)

Femi is Artistic Director of Tiata Fahodzi; Associate Director at West Yorkshire Playhouse, Leeds (2003) and Trainee Asso Director at the Royal Court (2003).

For Tiata Fahodzi: Tiata Delights, a festival play readings at Arcola Theatre, Dalston (2004) and national tours of Abyssinia (200 Makinde (2000), Bonded (1999) and Book (1998).

Other theatre includes: Medea, Off Camer (West Yorkshire Playhouse); Dealer's Choi (Salisbury Playhouse); Tickets & Ties (Thea Royal, Stratford East and Sweden); It's Goo to Talk (Theatre Royal, Stratford East).

As an actor: Marching for Fausa, The Stubb Corpse and Daughters (Royal Court).

Film includes: The Legend of 1900.

Future projects for Tiata Fahodzi include a revival of Wole Soyinka's The Lion and the Jewel (Spring 2005).

n Gilet

atre includes: Come Out Eli (The Actors
tre/Arcola); The Alchemist (Riverside); As
Like It (NT); Unfinished Business (Talawa);
s in the Band, Elegies (King's Head/West
); Clandestine Marriage (West End); As You
It, School for Scandal (Holland Park); Fences
glish Theatre, Frankfurt); Deserving Poor
ntameters Theatre); Robinson Crusoe
vilion Theatre, Glasgow); A Taste of Honey
ap Theatre Company).

vision includes: 55 Degrees North, The Bill,
ctors, Silent Witness, Babyfather, Single
es, Time Gentlemen Please – series 2,
ting It, Holby City, Casualty, Brothers and
ers, Dear Dilemma, Now What!, Punt and
inis, Firm Friends 11, Demob, Desmonds, Do
urself – Double Exposure, Wiz Bang – series
Nature of Science, Playabout, Pigsty.

includes: Wonderland Experience, Greasy,
me Run.

y Kerbel (assistant director)

y graduated with a first class degree in Drama
Theatre studies from Royal Holloway,
versity of London in 2003.

has previously assisted on play readings at
National Theatre, Theatre Royal, Stratford
and Stratford Circus.

ma Laxton (sound designer)

the Royal Court, Food Chain, Terrorism.
er theatre includes: My Dad is a Birdman
ung Vic); Party Time/One For The Road
C); As You Like It, Romeo and Juliet (Regent's
Open Air Theatre).

ma was Head of Sound at Regent's Park Open
Theatre in 2001 and 2002 where
jects included A Midsummer Night's Dream,
e's Labour's Lost, Where's Charley, The
tes Of Penzance and Oh! What A Lovely War.
ma has recently been on sabbatical at the
ional Theatre working with Complicite on
sure For Measure.

ma is Sound Deputy at the Royal Court.

Ultz (designer and lighting designer)

As designer, for the Royal Court: Young
Playwrights' Season 2004, Fallout, The Night
Heron, Fireface, Lift Off, Mojo (also at
Steppenwolf Theater, Chicago).
As designer, other theatre includes: sixteen
productions for the RSC including Good (also on
Broadway), The Art of Success (also at
Manhattan Theatre Club); The Black Prince, Me
and Mamie O' Rourke, A Madhouse in Goa,
Animal Crackers, When Harry Met Sally (West
End); Slavs! (Hampstead); The Resistible Rise of
Arturo Ui, Ramayana (RNT); Hobson's Choice
(Young Vic); Xerxes, La Clemenza di Tito,
The Rake's Progress, Die Entführung aus dem
Serail (Bavarian State Opera).
As director and designer, other theatre includes:
Summer Holiday (Blackpool Opera House,
London Apollo, UK tour, South African tour);
Jesus Christ Superstar (Aarhus and Copenhagen);
Don Giovanni, Cosi Fan Tutte (in Japanese for
Tokyo Globe); A Midsummer Night's Dream
(National Arts Centre, Ottawa); Dragon (RNT);
The Screens (California); The Maids, Deathwatch
(co-directed RSC); The Blacks (co-directed
Market Theatre Johannesburg and Stockholms
Stadsteater); Perikles (Stockholms Stadsteater);
Snowbull (Hampstead); L'Elisir D'Amore (Tiroler
Landes Theater); The Public, The Taming of the
Shrew, Pericles, Baiju Bawra, Da Boyz (Theatre
Royal, Stratford East).

Trevor Wallace (lighting designer)

For the Royal Court: Notes on Falling Leaves,
Rampage, A Day in Dull Armour, Graffitti.
Other theatre includes: Golden Boy, Nobody's
Perfect, The Book of the Banshee, Kit and the
Widow – The Fat Lady Sings (Yvonne Arnaud
Theatre, Guildford); Cabaret, Sweet Charity
(Electric Theatre, Guildford); The Changeling
(Sandpit Theatre, St Albans); Comedy of Errors,
Grimm Tales, Richard III, Cyrano de Bergerac,
Les Enfants du Paradis (Minack Theatre,
Cornwall).
Trevor is the Deputy Head of Lighting at the
Royal Court.

THE ENGLISH STAGE COMPANY AT THE ROYAL COURT

The English Stage Company at the Royal Court opened in 1956 as a subsidised theatre producing new British plays, international plays and some classical revivals.

The first artistic director George Devine aimed to create a writers' theatre, 'a place where the dramatist is acknowledged as the fundamental creative force in the theatre and where the play is more important than the actors, the director, the designer'. The urgent need was to find a contemporary style in which the play, the acting, direction and design are all combined. He believed that 'the battle will be a long one to continue to create the right conditions for writers to work in'.

Devine aimed to discover 'hard-hitting, uncompromising writers whose plays are stimulating, provocative and exciting'. The Royal Court production of John Osborne's Look Back in Anger in May 1956 is now seen as the decisive starting point of modern British drama and the policy created a new generation of British playwrights. The first wave included John Osborne, Arnold Wesker, John Arden, Ann Jellicoe, N F Simpson and Edward Bond. Early seasons included new international plays by Bertolt Brecht, Eugène Ionesco, Samuel Beckett, Jean-Paul Sartre and Marguerite Duras.

The theatre started with the 400-seat proscenium arch Theatre Downstairs, and then in 1969 opened a second theatre, the 60-seat studio Theatre Upstairs. Some productions transfer to the West End, such as Terry Johnson's Hitchcock Blonde, Caryl Churchill's Far Away, Conor McPherson's The Weir, Kevin Elyot's Mouth to Mouth and My Night With Reg. The Royal Court also co-produces plays which have transferred to the West End or toured internationally, such as Sebastian Barry's The Steward of Christendom and Mark Ravenhill's Shopping and Fucking (with Out of Joint), Martin McDonagh's The Beauty Queen Of Leenane (with Druid Theatre Company), Ayub Khan-Din's East is East (with Tamasha Theatre Company, and now a feature film).

Since 1994 the Royal Court's artistic policy has again been vigorously directed to finding and producing a new generation of playwrights. The writers include Joe Penhall, Rebecca Prichard, Michael Wynne, Nick Grosso, Judy Upton, Meredith Oakes, Sarah Kane, Anthony Neilson, Judith Johnson, James Stock, Jez Butterworth, Marina Carr, Phyllis Nagy, Simon Block, Martin McDonagh, Mark Ravenhill, Ayub Khan-Din, Tamantha Hammerschlag, Jess Walters, Ché Walker, Conor McPherson,

Simon Stephens, Richard Bean, Roy Williams, Gary Mitchell, Mick Mahoney, Rebecca Gilma. Christopher Shinn, Kia Corthron, David Gieselmann, Marius von Mayenburg, David Eldridge, Leo Butler, Zinnie Harris, Grae Cleu Enda Walsh, Roland Schimmelpfennig, DeObi Oparei, Vassily Sigarev, the Presnyakov Broth Marcos Barbosa and Lucy Prebble. This expanded programme of new plays has been made possible through the support of A.S.K Theater Projects and the Skirball Foundation, Jerwood Charitable Foundation, the America Friends of the Royal Court Theatre and many association with the Royal National Theatre Studio.

In recent years there have been record-break productions at the box office, with capacity houses for Roy Williams' Fallout, Terry Johnso Hitchcock Blonde, Caryl Churchill's A Numbe Jez Butterworth's The Night Heron, Rebecca Gilman's Boy Gets Girl, Kevin Elyot's Mouth Mouth, David Hare's My Zinc Bed and Conor McPherson's The Weir, which transferred to West End in October 1998 and ran for nearly two years at the Duke of York's Theatre.

The newly refurbished theatre in Sloane Squa opened in February 2000, with a policy still inspired by the first artistic director George Devine. The Royal Court is an international theatre for new plays and new playwrights, a the work shapes contemporary drama in Brit and overseas.

WARDS FOR
HE ROYAL COURT

z Butterworth won the 1995 George Devine
vard, the Writers' Guild New Writer of the
ar Award, the Evening Standard Award for
ost Promising Playwright and the Olivier
ward for Best Comedy for Mojo.

ne Royal Court was the overall winner of the
•95 Prudential Award for the Arts for
eativity, excellence, innovation and accessibility.
ne Royal Court Theatre Upstairs won the 1995
ter Brook Empty Space Award for innovation
d excellence in theatre.

ichael Wynne won the 1996 Meyer-Whitworth
ward for The Knocky. Martin McDonagh won
e 1996 George Devine Award, the 1996
riters' Guild Best Fringe Play Award, the 1996
ritics' Circle Award and the 1996 Evening
andard Award for Most Promising Playwright
r The Beauty Queen of Leenane. Marina Carr
on the 19th Susan Smith Blackburn Prize
996/7) for Portia Coughlan. Conor McPherson
on the 1997 George Devine Award, the 1997
ritics' Circle Award and the 1997 Evening
andard Award for Most Promising Playwright
r The Weir. Ayub Khan-Din won the 1997
riters' Guild Awards for Best West End Play
d Writers' Guild New Writer of the Year and
e 1996 John Whiting Award for East is East
o-production with Tamasha).

: the 1998 Tony Awards, Martin McDonagh's
ne Beauty Queen of Leenane (co-production
ith Druid Theatre Company) won four awards
cluding Garry Hynes for Best Director and was
ominated for a further two. Eugene Ionesco's
ne Chairs (co-production with Theatre de
omplicite) was nominated for six Tony awards.
avid Hare won the 1998 Time Out Live Award
r Outstanding Achievement and six awards in
ew York including the Drama League, Drama
esk and New York Critics Circle Award for Via
olorosa. Sarah Kane won the 1998 Arts
oundation Fellowship in Playwriting. Rebecca
ichard won the 1998 Critics' Circle Award for
ost Promising Playwright for Yard Gal (co-
oduction with Clean Break).

onor McPherson won the 1999 Olivier Award
r Best New Play for The Weir. The Royal
ourt won the 1999 ITI Award for Excellence in
ternational Theatre. Sarah Kane's Cleansed
as judged Best Foreign Language Play in 1999
 Theater Heute in Germany. Gary Mitchell
on the 1999 Pearson Best Play Award for
ust. Rebecca Gilman was joint winner of the 1999
999 George Devine Award and won the 1999
vening Standard Award for Most Promising
aywright for The Glory of Living.

In 1999, the Royal Court won the European
theatre prize New Theatrical Realities,
presented at Taormina Arte in Sicily, for its
efforts in recent years in discovering and
producing the work of young British dramatists.

Roy Williams and Gary Mitchell were joint
winners of the George Devine Award 2000 for
Most Promising Playwright for Lift Off and The
Force of Change respectively. At the Barclays
Theatre Awards 2000 presented by the TMA,
Richard Wilson won the Best Director Award for
David Gieselmann's Mr Kolpert and Jeremy
Herbert won the Best Designer Award for Sarah
Kane's 4.48 Psychosis. Gary Mitchell won the
Evening Standard's Charles Wintour Award 2000
for Most Promising Playwright for The Force of
Change. Stephen Jeffreys' I Just Stopped by to
See The Man won an AT&T: On Stage Award
2000.

David Eldridge's Under the Blue Sky won the
Time Out Live Award 2001 for Best New Play in
the West End. Leo Butler won the George
Devine Award 2001 for Most Promising
Playwright for Redundant. Roy Williams won the
Evening Standard's Charles Wintour Award 2001
for Most Promising Playwright for Clubland.
Grae Cleugh won the 2001 Olivier Award for
Most Promising Playwright for Fucking Games.
Richard Bean was joint winner of the George
Devine Award 2002 for Most Promising
Playwright for Under the Whaleback. Caryl
Churchill won the 2002 Evening Standard Award
for Best New Play for A Number. Vassily Sigarev
won the 2002 Evening Standard Charles Wintour
Award for Most Promising Playwright for
Plasticine. Ian MacNeil won the 2002 Evening
Standard Award for Best Design for A Number
and Plasticine. Peter Gill won the 2002 Critics'
Circle Award for Best New Play for The York
Realist (English Touring Theatre). Ché Walker
won the 2003 George Devine Award for Most
Promising Playwright for Flesh Wound. Lucy
Prebble won the 2003 Critics' Circle Award for
Most Promising Playwright and the 2004 George
Devine Award for Most Promising Playwright for
The Sugar Syndrome.

ROYAL COURT BOOKSHOP

The Royal Court Bookshop offers a range of
contemporary plays and publications on the
theory and practice of modern drama. The staff
specialise in assisting with the selection of
audition monologues and scenes.
Royal Court playtexts from past and present
productions cost £2.
The Bookshop is situated in the downstairs Royal
Court Bar and Food.
Monday – Friday 3-10pm, Saturday 2-10pm
For information tel: 020 7565 5024 or email:
bookshop@royalcourttheatre.com

ROYAL COURT
SLOANE SQUARE

Jerwood Theatre Upstairs
YOUNG PLAYWRIGHTS' SEASON 2004

A Genesis Project

Design: Ultz.

1 – 30 October
THE WEATHER
by **Clare Pollard**
Directed by Ramin Gray

Cast includes: Alex Robertson, Helen Schlesinger and Mia Soteriou.

5 – 16 October
BEAR HUG
by **Robin French**
Directed by Ramin Gray

Cast includes: Helen Schlesinger.

5 – 20 November
FRESH KILLS
by **Elyzabeth Gregory Wilder**
Directed by Wilson Milam

26 November – 18 December
A GIRL IN A CAR WITH A MAN
by **Rob Evans**
Directed by Joe Hill-Gibbins

Cast includes: Mark Bonnar.

BOX OFFICE 020 7565 5000
BOOK ONLINE
www.royalcourttheatre.com

ARTS COUNCIL ENGLAND

John Donnelly
Bone

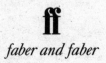

faber and faber

First published in 2004
by Faber and Faber Limited
3 Queen Square London WC1N 3AU

Typeset by Country Setting, Kingsdown, Kent CT14 8ES
Printed in England by Mackays of Chatham plc, Chatham, Kent

A CIP record for this book
is available from the British Library

ISBN 0-571-22715-5

2 4 6 8 10 9 7 5 3 1

Acknowledgements

Love and thanks are always due to

Mum, for the colouring pencils

All you good good people, for your love,
prayers, support, encouragement and
somewhere to sleep safe at night

Most generous God, for this and more

All at Interplay, especially Lauren, Brett, and Mark

All you cats at the Court, especially Joe,
Graham, Charlotte, and Slim

The very beautiful people at The Site

Jonathan and Cathy Kearney

Chris Thorpe

And of course, the late Niels Wangerin,
much loved mentor and friend

Have yourselves a glass of wine.
Maybe two glasses. Maybe three

Please support your local charities,
Amnesty International, and maketradefair.com

JD, August 2004

God breathes through us so completely . . .
So gently we hardly feel it . . . yet,
It is our everything.

John Coltrane

Author's Note

A director must find a coherent place where all three characters can exist together. They must not be isolated from one another onstage, for instance, by altering lighting each time a different character speaks. This does not mean that all characters must be equally lit at all times.

They are on the verge of something vast, perhaps facing out to sea.

The characters must never address one another or interact directly. But occasionally they might betray an awareness of one another's presence – something akin to experiencing the sensation that there is someone else in the room, only to discover that you are alone.

The characters must connect on an emotional level. Occasionally, this emotional or spiritual connection is overt.

Parentheses are sometimes used to indicate a change in intention or direction on the part of the speaker when this might otherwise be unclear – for instance, if a character interrupts herself with a new thought or addresses a new person for part of a line.

Towards the end of the play, the rhythm of the lines should ebb and flow, the lines lapping at one another like waves. During the course of the play the lighting increases, almost imperceptibly, until the final state, as indicated.

Characters

Helen
late fifties, white

Stephen
mid thirties, black

Jamie
early twenties, white

(*ages are guidelines*)

BONE

I must arise now and go about the city;
In the streets and in the squares
I must seek him whom my soul loves.

Song of Solomon

Stephen, Helen, Jamie onstage.

Helen (*sharp intake of breath*)

  Lights down. Lights up.

Helen (*sharp intake of breath*)

  Lights down. Lights up.

Helen (*with a start*) Gunshots and screaming, hear the pop and crackle of fat and bone. The scent of pyres hangs in the air like stale incense. Waves upon waves of lambs rise up over the hills and there are gunners stationed in the houses, mowing them down, one wave after another, and as the bodies hit the ground they decay almost instantly and ignite, filling the land with fire and smoke till –

  Lights down. Lights up.

You undress me. Your hands on me. Your breath. Your heat. Your weight. Your – (*Sharp intake of breath.*)

  Lights down. Lights up.

Alone again. I smooth the sheet next to me. Smoke from the pyres drifts in through the windows. I'd close them but it's so hot. I'd cry but I'm too tired. Sometimes I'll lie here for hours. Not awake. Not asleep. Somewhere in –

  Lights down. Lights up.

I'm in a bath with you. It's warm. You're soaping my back and your arms are around me. Sunlight streams in through the open windows. Then you lean past me, pull

the plug out and the water pours down the drain. I shift
forward, try and put it back in, but you hold me back,
you won't let me. The water's going, I struggle and fight
but you're too strong and I watch, helpless, as the last of
the water pours away. The water's all gone. It's cold now.
And I'm – (*Sharp intake of breath.*)

Lights down. Lights up.

I close the door of the medicine cabinet and stare at the
woman in the mirror. Feel the bags under her eyes. When
did you get so old? Close my eyes.

Stephen I feel your pain.

Lights down. Lights up.

Helen I put the kettle on. Take two mugs from the tree.
Put one back. Force of habit. Through the kitchen
window I see the pyres stretching across the fields. No
stars in the sky. Smoke's too thick, it gets everywhere,
in my clothes, my hair. No matter how hard I scrub it
won't go – there's a star! Up there. Make a wish. Kettle's
whistling. Dog's asleep in his basket. Smell of burnt flesh
fills my nostrils.

Lights down. Lights up.

My tea's cold. The pyres are still burning but not so
frightening with the light. Dog's wagging his tail, making
a fuss. I stroke him, ruffle his coat. Rub his tummy. Kiss
his head. Fetch a tin of food and mix it with the grey
pellets from under the sink. Good boy. Good boy.
Something else, but I'm not sure what. Open a drawer.
Scissors, tape, string, no. Close. Try another, knives and –
no. Plates, cups, saucers, no. Try under the sink again.
Pick up the polish, no, that's not – white spirit behind the
bleach. Yes. Take out the container, put it on the kitchen
table. Open another drawer. Your lighter. Set it down
next to the white spirit. Yes, that's it. That's right. Shake

the tub of pills. Empty. Cross to the fridge, unscrew your whisky, take a swig. And another. And . . . that's it . . . that's it . . . I sit down. Close my eyes. And wait. Finally it comes.

Stephen I feel your pain. Because I have felt it too. And I have found the solution.

Lights up. Lights down.

Helen Today is going to be a good day. I can feel it in my bones.

Stephen Alarm goes. Seven-o-one. Voice on the radio tells me three soldiers were killed last night by a suicide bomber and that farming thing's still going on. I should listen really, I try and pay attention, but next thing I know it's eighteen minutes past and a song's playing.

Helen Lift my coat from the hook by the door, step over the dog, bang my knee on the washing machine – ow – and head out to the Volvo. Pop into town, get my back pills and a card for Janey. She's twelve on Tuesday, so if I post it today it should get there. Open the door, climb in, key in ignition. Deep breath. Last chance. Turn the key and –

Stephen In the shower feel my balls for lumps, but I don't really know what I'm looking for.

Jamie My stiffy is raging.

Helen Road into town's quiet. Think I'll adjust the visor flap. Sun's so bright, I'm getting a headache from the – that's better . . . Lovely drive, though, uninterrupted country, no fences anywhere. Just occasional piles of rubble where the walls were before we knocked them down, those bloody movement restrictions. Turn the radio on, something about the war, Christ not more death, turn it off. No escape from it. Pull off into the doctor's office.

Jamie Horn like a rhinoceros, you could hang a flag off this, in fact I will! I'll wrap it up in St George, put it on display, and all the people will flock from miles around – the Queen, the England football captain, Elton John, all to marvel at my tremendous erection. Great, seething crowds will gather and, somewhere down the front, a father will turn to his boy and, with a lump in his throat, say, now that, my son, is a British cock.

Helen Girl on reception didn't half make a fuss. I mean, it's only a bloody week, it's not that big a deal is it? I said, the pills don't work any more, what can I do? I need to take extra. They gave it to me anyway, so I don't know what they were moaning about. Suppose they've got to be careful. Can't just dole them out, never know what might happen.

Jamie Tend to wake up with a blinder after a good kip. Consider knocking one off but nah – save it for later. Some lucky darling's in for a treat.

Stephen Bit of product in the hair for that sleek, well-groomed look, a look that says, I'm in control of my hair – ergo, my life. Suited and booted, ready to rock.

Jamie Other hand, nothing like cleaning the pipes first thing. Maybe I will have a quick go.

Stephen Bright morning sun streams into the kitchen and I'm in coffee heaven. And sorry, I stopped buying the Fairtrade. I mean I don't mind paying over the odds so Pedro can send his kids to school but it does seem a bit rich when five-year-olds on three pence a day can make a decent cup and Pedro's coffee tastes like bum-muck. Right. Keys?

Jamie Like I say, belter like this, be a shame to let it gohhhhhhhhhh blimey there go the knees.

Stephen Come on, you itinerant metal bastards, where are you hiding?

Helen Pony, no, that's a bit twee. What about this one? David Beckham? Think she's getting a bit old for him. There's nothing here. Get an arty one, she likes art. There we are. All right if I borrow your counter? Ta. Have a great day. Lots of love. Auntie Helen.

Jamie Marmite on toast. No. Yes. No. Coco Puffs. Yes.

Stephen Think! Where did you have them last?

Jamie Necklace, wallet, mobile, keys.

Stephen Keys!

Jamie Check wallet for johnnies (can't be too careful, d'you know what I mean?) Underpants, one pair, clean, suitable for eyes of a lady, and one ironed uniform, courtesy of Sis (sorry, that girl's a fuckin angel). All laid out on the bed, all present and correct.

Stephen Stay calm and you will find them, stay calm and you will – oh for cock's sake! (Oh, here we are, behind the lava lamp next to a picture of us in the Alps.)

Helen I was amazed how much Janey's grown when I last saw her. She was lovely, bless her, didn't really know what to say. Neither did your sister, or Geoff, but still, they made an effort, which was nice. She's turning into a proper young lady is Janey. She'll be turning heads soon. Actually, rate kids grow up these days I bet she's doing more than that already. Whole life ahead of her. Unlike some. Postbox outside the chemist.

Stephen Oh, and there's your copy of 'The Waste Land', I keep meaning to return that. It's not bad, actually, I have a flick every now and then, appeals to my feminine side. I'd post it but we should probably meet up for coffee or something. More friendly.

Jamie Case packed, ready for departure. Time check. High noon.

Stephen Pack the essentials into my faux-leather case (your present to me four years ago), about to leave the house when I notice my neighbour locking his door and knowing he also uses the Tube I hang back to avoid a conversation. (*as if watching him go*) The two great unanswered questions of the modern age – who is God and who lives next door? Okay, that should do. Earphones in, in case someone gets chatty and –

Jamie Little Sis, you'll be glad to hear, is doing well, under the circumstances – it's been traumatic, you understand, not just for her, for all of us.

Stephen Hold my case in my left hand, Oyster card nestling in my right hip-pocket. Approach the ticket barrier, lift the card from my pocket with my right hand, swipe and pass through the barrier in one clean motion, taking pride in the fact I neither vary my speed nor touch the sides of the barrier with my case. I am so the man.

Jamie You all right, babe? Got everything you need? Mum been to see you? . . . Don't surprise me, I haven't seen her neither – shacked up somewhere, no doubt, no no no, babe, you sit yourself . . . well, cup of tea'd be nice.

Stephen Now. Pay attention. Tube door normally opens here, about a foot in from the right-hand edge of that poster and this carriage stops right by the exit sign ready for when I get off the other end. Doors open, sidestep a backpacker and I'm on. You see, a yard's miscalculation either way and, my friend, you're . . . oh, this is all I need.

Jamie Sis needs a bit of lookin' after. I left her, laid up on the sofa, cheeks aglow like an angel, reading the *Hello!* I bought for her. She was getting all flappy what with tomorrow, me off and everythin', kept fussing after me, she's my little angel, she really is. Would've told her not to, but she needs summin, y'know, take her mind off (makes me so fucking angry) . . . Think I'll send her a text, keep her spirits up.

Helen While they make up the prescription, I chat to Daniel, you remember Daniel, young lad, works there weekends, always round the lanes on his bike. I ask him if he's got a girlfriend yet? Still working on it, he says. Well, if you need anyone to practise on, I say, you give me a call! She may be old but she's still in working order! He smiles a little and blushes. Warmth in my chest takes me by surprise. As he hands over the little paper bag, our fingers brush and I notice he has strong hands like yours.

Stephen An incident is in progress. As the door closes, an unshaven black guy shoves his way on, swearing, smelling, and as he does so he shoulders a white girl in the face. She calls him a wanker. He asks her who she's calling a wanker. She tells him who she's calling a wanker.

Helen For some reason this makes me think of our wedding night. Seeing you naked for the first time, I was so . . . (funny). I start the car and pull away.

Jamie SIS. DONT WORY BOUT ME. WILL PULL A NICE 1! THNKNG OF U. CU 1ST THNG. KISSHUG KISSHUG.

Helen I remember you holding my face in your hand, a hand so big I thought it could hold the world. You traced a line across my cheek with your thumb, down my neck, loosening the strap from – shit!

Jamie What the fuck!

Stephen Suddenly, a white guy steps in and, oh my God, he tells the black guy to watch his fucking mouth and the entire carriage chokes on its liberal cornflakes. Is the white guy doing this because the other guy's black? Because the girl's pretty and he wants to cop off with her? S'pose he could just be a nice bloke.

Helen Where did he come from? He just stepped out in front of me.

Jamie Want to watch where you're going!

Helen You were on your phone, you weren't even looking where you're going. Bloody idiot, I could have killed you.

Stephen He's right in her face and, fair play, she's giving it back but he's twice her size and oh shit, I'm going to have to do something. Okay, just leave it a few seconds, maybe it'll calm down on its own.

Jamie Cunt.

Stephen That'll be a no, then. Maybe I should do something.

Helen Stares at me like he's going to thump me, bloody nerve, like to see him try.

Stephen Voyeurism. The thinking man's masturbation. Who needs porn when you've got the Tube?

Jamie Oi! What you looking at, wanker?

Stephen Oop. Eye-contact. Look away.

Helen Bloody little idiot.

Jamie Yes, cunt, you.

Helen He walks off and I drive. Why do people do that? It's like the whole world's filled with hate.

Stephen Black guy alights at Elephant, whole Tube breathes a sigh of relief. The girl thanks the white guy (which reminds me, did you see that thing in *Time Out*?

Apparently over sixty per cent of conversations start over how much of a twat someone else is. Anyway, she's pretty (in a kooky kind of way), reminds me of you actually. The guy asks the girl for her number. She gives it and I feel a surge of –

Helen No, it's nothing, really, it's nothing, just that man, I'm . . . Sorry, I've got to stop the car . . . I'm fine, I said, I'm fine. Let's just get home. Goodness' sake, fuss.

Jamie At the pub, relate the story of the old bloke in the Citroën and the nerve of that kid, staring at me after I almost been run over. The lads as you can imagine are outraged. So much so they buy me another round. Quarter past three.

Helen No, I'm fine, really, it's nothing, it's . . . silly. Just give me a moment. (*Exhales.*) Wouldn't do that if you were around.

Stephen I swear I was this close to saying something, I was just gauging the situation. Walking north over London Bridge, I replay the incident, except this time I'm the guy who steps in. I imagine handling the black guy with dignity and aplomb, that I get the kooky girl's phone number. And in my mind I fix her with a wry smile and in front of the entire carriage say – hey. How about you and me call in sick, do something crazy? And she giggles and brushes her hair and swaying her shoulders a little says – sure. Why not? And we walk by the river and eat icecream and catch a black-and-white movie and share a day so perfect that later we can't help but go back to her bohemian loft conversion (she's an artist) and make love tenderly until dawn. And then it's years later I'm outside the Film Theatre café on the South Bank. Tap on my shoulder, look up, and it's you, and it's great to see you, it really is. Yeah, yeah, things are good, actually, and I ask you how you are, and there's sadness in your eyes and you tell me that not a day goes by you don't think of me and that you're sorry things didn't work out and there's something you need to ask, and then at that precise moment the kooky girl appears from the café carrying two glasses of white wine, and I say, Sarah, this is my wife, Catherine, and – the fuck is this guy's problem? . . . Midway over the river some drunk sprawled on the pavement nearly sends me flying. Puke-stained suit, dry blood on his face, raging at the air, fists clenched, something about today being a good day? As I pass he grins like he knows something I don't, like, y'know, the way on TV homeless people are always strangely wise? But actually that's bollocks. They're just mental.

Jamie Ten to eight, place is crawling with trim. Marks out of ten? I'd give her one. We all laugh. Then Mickey pipes up. 'Ere, mate, she looks a bit like your sister! A hush descends. Quick as a flash, I'm there. He's apologising before I even touch him, knows he's bang out of line – sorry, mate, sorry, didn't think, he says. Hands round his throat, you what you what you fucking what did you say? I don't think he meant anything by it, mate, easy. That's Alex – good-looking bastard, swarthy, gets his share. I let go. Don't want to spoil the occasion. I know you didn't mean anything, mate, just a bit sensitive that's all. No, no, no, he says. Not after what your sister been through. 'Ere, this one's on us. Two doormen appear, big bastards, obviously seen the fracas – everything all right, lads? Yeah, lads' night out, says Alex, bit of fun between mates, that's all (you got to hand it to him). Special occasion, the taller one says? As a matter of fact it is, says Terry, with (I don't mind saying) a hint of pride. This lad's off in the morning fight for his country. Turns out taller one's seen active service with the paddies. Any advice? I say. Yeah, he says, don't get shot.

Helen Quiet as I step out the car. No barking, which seems odd till I remember I poisoned the dog. Step over the dog as I come in the back. Bin's full so I remove the sack, tie the strings, step back over the dog, bang my knee again on the washer. Ow!

Stephen Shit! Forgot to call Dad last night.

Helen Open the door with one hand, carry the sack to the wheelie bin, open the lid, chuck it. Close the bin, knock the dirt from my hands, return indoors, right. Do this bloody paper-work, then pot of tea.

Stephen Lifts fill me with dread – Fifth floor, please. What if you start a conversation and the lift breaks down? What if you had to talk to these people for ever?

Jamie Ten-fifteen. Okay. I admit it. I'm a ladies' man. Twelve pints in me, and I could still satisfy two ladies at the same time. Captain Quim they call me, the Quimmaster General, Dr Quim Medicine Woman, Russell Crowe: Master and Quimmander. I am Lord of the Quim. Seriously though, think I might be one o' them sex addicts. It's a medical condition – celebrities get it (well), between you and me, I think they just can't keep it in their pants, but you know these doctors. Any old half-baked bollocks, before you know it, they'll have you up on a couch crying how you was touched up by the dodgy uncle you never had. But me, I ain't got no issues, I'm just hungry for the minge, insatiable appetite, and yes, like Scott of the Antarctic, on occasion I have been known to make the long voyage South.

Helen I've got a list. I do lots of lists, it's the only way I can get things done. Number one on my list is always write a list. No, it sounds silly, but it means as soon as I've written my list, I can tick something off, then it's like a, y'know, but it means I've achieved something . . . You think I'm barmy, don't you? Well, it helps me. Number two. Pay the bills. Three. Defrost the freezer. Four –

Stephen Ding! This is me. Marketing. Greet my staff with confidence, stride into my office with pride, close the door behind me, sit at my desk and look up at the framed sign bearing the three Fs, the company's unofficial mantra, the holy grail of the sale. Feel. Felt. Found. I feel your pain. Because I have felt it too. And I have found the solution. I log on to my computer, stare at the screen and weep at how shit my life is. Hey. Joking.

Helen It's funny, I don't mind it any more, all this paper-work. I actually find it calms me. Hang on, what's that asking me? . . . I do it all now, all the bills, gas, electric, water, balance sheets, everything, I'm actually quite good at it. Most of the time. Mean, like I say, it's a learning curve and FUCK! (*Pause, calm.*) Sorry, sometimes . . . I don't know why, I just get . . . That was silly, just broke your mug. That was silly. It would have been nice if you'd left some instructions. Y'know, told me how to do some things. Before you left. Still. No point, y'know . . . God, my hands are shaking.

Jamie Little trick o' mine, never fails to get me served. Darling, darling, did it hurt? When, says the barmaid? When you fell from heaven, while you're at it, love, four pints of lager – ah shit, she's moved on.

Helen Grab your whisky from on top of the fridge, one of your tumblers from the cabinet next to the clock. Ten to three already, have to get a – take the paper bag from my handbag, open these . . . bloody child-caps, adult-caps more like, need hands like a navvy to shut up! . . . Goodness sake, stop talking, woman! Right. Pour the contents onto the kitchen table, arrange the pills into neat lines of eight. Fill a tumbler with whisky, knock back a line of pills and drink. More pills then drink, hold my breath, screw my eyes shut, and count, clenching my hands into fists . . . (*Counts under her breath then, when she can hold on no longer, inhales, exhales, reaching for* *breath*.) Still trembling. Pour another glass, another line, dig my nails in my palms and . . . (*Inhales, exhales, reaching for breath*.) Blood runs out from the centre of my palms over my wrists. Breathing. That's better. Is this it? I stare at my hand no idea how long, till it drifts out of focus and it's no longer a hand but a landscape, every crease and fold a valley or hill, a world in miniature. Hands are still now. Light from the window through my fingers. This it? No, need something, something else. Feeling in my gut, like an umbilical cord attached and someone's tugging (is it –?) and I'm up, following, up the stairs, like in a dream, into the bathroom, fling open the cabinet, throwing things aside, pills, bandages. What am I looking for? Tell me what I'm – Your hair-clippers, on the side. Of course. I pick them up.

Jamie Finally. Space clears at the bar, I'm up to the mark, elbow to the fore, waving a twenty like I'm the Queen, eye-contact, no messing this time. Then, just when I'm teetering on the precipice of liquid relief –

Helen Grey curls float to the bathroom floor. Feels strange. Doesn't feel real. I think of shearing sheep. I see them, herded into the pen, but this time it's not for shearing. The soldiers are here and they lead them out in pairs and –

Jamie What you mean, that's your lot? Don't give me that, I been here ten minutes!

Stephen I re-read (*present tense*) your e-mail from last week, yeah, sorry I couldn't make it along, just one of those things, I'm sure it all went off well. Should probably delete it but can't really be arsed so I move it to the folder with your name on it and purely 'cause I'm so bored I open the folder and scroll down your collected electronic works.

Jamie Last orders? Last –? What last orders? I didn't hear any last orders!

Stephen Blimey, they add up, don't they . . . Blimey!

Jamie Settle down? Settle – I'm off to fight a fucking war tomorrow, you're telling me to settle down? I'll settle you down, you cunt, you settle down, and before you know it, me and the boys are out on the street courtesy of Mr Active Service.

Stephen Open a couple of old ones just for old times' sake, I keep meaning to bin these but, y'know, just 'cause we're not . . . it doesn't mean, I mean it's not like that just negates – that's a nice one . . . Dad asks after you by the way, asks if I ever see you, I mean you were so good when Mum died, I mean, I know it was almost a year ago now, but still . . . anyway, he's doing all right, y'know, misses her but . . . Yeah, I think I'll delete these. I'll just go through some of them in case there's any, y'know, photos or useful information.

Jamie What's a man got to do for a drink round here? Country's going to the dogs, mate, I tell ya. 'S sake.

Helen On the way back into the kitchen I catch sight of a strange woman with a shaved head in the hallway mirror. I stop and ask her if this is it, but she just mouths the same words back.

Stephen Over lunch, and two glasses of wine (hey, let's throw caution to the wind), I toss last night's suicide bomb into the conversation like a poker-player throwing in his ante. I mention my third-hand opinions on the war with an air of weary concern and a shaking of the head that I hope denotes both compassion and a searching, humanitarian spirit. It seems to do the trick 'cause the new girl from executive accounts smiles at me. I smile back and make a mental note to pay more attention to the news. You'd know, what was the name of that important new play about the war? Got a great write-up though the guy reviewing it did sound like a bit of a wanker. Maybe I'll take her.

24

Helen I finish the pills with the rest of the whisky and sit and finish the paperwork. That's much better, much clearer now. Seems so funny this form. Writing down all I own. A fridge. A toaster. Hardly the bloody jackpot, is it? No one to leave it to, anyway, apart from Janey, really. Don't fancy your bloody sister getting her hands on it, though. I'm not blaming you, Tom, I knew we couldn't have kids, I'm just saying. But then we did, didn't we? Lots of them. Hundreds. Until the soldiers came and killed them. They killed my babies and then they killed you. Close my eyes I hear their screams, smell their flesh burning, did I tell you I have to live with that? Every night. Still, no complaints. Head out towards the west field and the metal sheds. Collect your lighter and the white spirit, step over the dog, bang my knee on the washing machine. Ow.

Jamie En route to New York's, stop off at Hassan's dog-meat emporium, line the old stomach. Seriously, you got to look after yourself on a night like this, otherwise things are liable to get out of hand.

Helen Cross the steading, pass the lambing sheds on the right. Hey, you remember Henry, that little lamb? Named him after Henry Cooper, the boxer. But he lost, you said. I know, but he tried, I said.

Stephen Shall I tell you about my working afternoon? You'll notice I spared you the gory details of the morning, suffice to say it was the usual gay carousel of screensavers, e-mails and mild sexual fantasies. Hang on, phone's going . . . Dad. Can't face him now. Voicemail. Have another look at your e-mail, nothing else to do. Knock off a quick reply. Thanks for your e-mail – no, that's a bit formal.

Helen Henry's mother had triplets so we had to set him on to another ewe with a spare teat. Coated him in his new mum's fluids, so she'd take to him. Bloody mess that was! Beautiful little thing. You told me I was being soppy giving him a name but don't think I don't know you were out here every night, checking on him. Shame he didn't make it. You always did pretend not to care, said it was girly. Said the same thing about that pink shirt I bought you. Wore it, though. Remember that time we went up to London, we saw that Monument, the one they built for the people who died in the fire? I said I thought it was good they did that then. You said it was –

Stephen Okay, how's this sound. Hi . . . hi. Good to hear from you . . . Really good to hear from you (yup). Sorry I couldn't make it. Like I said, had another wedding to go to. Hope married life treating you well. Must dash. Up to my eyes, kiss, Steve . . . no, looks a bit . . . Love, Steve, no. No! Comma – comma, Steve, no that looks fucking – ohhh fuck it! This is ridiculous. 'Kiss, Steve' it's standard. Right . . . the little arrow hovers over the send button . . . Have you noticed how there's a kind of weird symmetry to how much attention you pay to the signing off part of e-mails and texts at the beginning and end of relationships . . . ? Annnnd click. I delete the e-mail.

Helen That sky's threatening something. It's muggy, going to throw it down soon, I'll bet. See Daniel heading along the north lane on his bike. Must be on his way home from work. That time already? Sees me and waves. I wave back and he slows down, freewheels, looking towards me a few seconds as if thinking about coming over. He pedals off. You'd look nice in those jeans.

Stephen Well, late afternoon, suppose I'd better do some work. There's been a complaint about the new futures and securities brochure, apparently the typeface isn't clear (the 'I' looks like a 'Y', I won't bore you). Technically this is my fault – I approved it – but no way I'm taking the rap. Can you send Ken in, please?

Helen In all honesty, it's been quite liberating actually, not having you around. Made me more independent. Made me realise the things I can do.

Stephen While I wait I think about Stephanie, the new girl from accounts, I think I might have mentioned her (?) I close my eyes and start to undress her.

Helen Y'know, like the paperwork for instance, which is fine, and running this place, though it does get a bit much sometimes.

Stephen Moves her hand round the small of my back, I kiss the dip above her –

Helen Though I have to say I haven't really done much with it for a couple of months. Joe was good. He kept coming round even after I couldn't afford to pay him. Eventually, though, there was nothing left to do. It's funny, what with you not being around, made me realise that . . .

Stephen I love you, Sarah, I mean Stephanie.

Helen . . . you know I'd always thought I was such a part of this place, you know, part of the community. We'd see people, and we had friends. But, when you left, I . . . well, I – it's funny, but, it made me realise that, well, I don't actually know these people. They're not really my friends. They're your friends, not mine. Again, I'm not blaming you. They were good, I mean, they invited me over, but . . . no one knew what to say, and that's when it dawned on me, that everything came through you.

Stephen Your mouth on my stomach my hands stroking the back of your – Ken! Come in. No, no, no, not interrupting anything. No, this shouldn't take long.

Jamie Got to watch the Turks, bunch of psychos. Not being racist, it's true and I respect 'em for it. Remember a few years back, some of their boys killed a couple of our boys over the football? Northern wankers, as it happens, northern boys never was much cop in a scrap, but at the end of the day, when it's us against them, it's different, isn't it? Now, say this, 'cause ever since I been chatting up this sweet little blonde bit, matey over there – must be the brother of the owner or something, fuck-all idea what else he thinks he's playing at, 'cause he ain't working, all he's doing is sitting there minding the skewers – ever since I been sweet-talking blondie, matey's been giving me the eye – wo wo wo – easy on the chilli-sauce, Hassan, don't want the shits on a troopship. Anyway. So. Hassan's on horse-meat duty (no, fuck the salad), matey's giving me the eye. I gesture to the lads (you'll love this), an' I say, hey boys. This cunt's giving me the eye. 'S he bent or what? Whole place creases up.

Stephen Ken, this should be an 'I', it looks like a 'Y' for goodness sakes, there is no 'Y' in securities, only 'I'. Two 'I's. You see? You do? Because these securities don't, you know why? Because they've got no 'I's.

Jamie 'Is he bent or what?'! D'you hear that? Magic!

Stephen Yes, I appreciate that, Ken, but I would have expected a modicum of common – (and on it goes). Fifteen years my senior he has to take this crap from me. I tell Ken how bad a job he's done. About the errors his team has made. I tell him he's incompetent, a disgrace, hoping, praying he'll do something, tell me to shove my job, anything, because, Ken, if you don't, fifteen years down the line, that's me in that chair getting a bollocking from some prick in an off-the-peg suit. But he just sits there, taking all my lies and evasions.

Jamie So, money paid, nice bit of banter with blondie, I'm all set to blame it on the boogie with the pussy posse – we're done (or so I think). 'Cause all of a sudden, matey pipes up. You what? I'm like De Niro in *Taxi Driver*. You talking to me? Well I don't know who else you're talking to, 'cause I'm the only one here (well, me and three mates, as it happens). Yes, wanker, you, don't get all coy now (he's scared now, matey, Turkish bloke). What you saying? Should treat her better, he says, shouldn't talk to her like that. What, I say, you telling me how to treat women? You lot treat your women like fucking animals!

Stephen When did this happen? I never used to be like this. I used to care about things.

Jamie Get out my shop, he says! Always drunk, always the same! No problem, mate, I've had enough of you, and your stinking dog meat. 'S not dog meat, he says. This good fresh meat. Yeah, I say, I seen you leading stray dogs round the back to stick on that thing, but not before you give them a good seeing to, you dog-fucker.

Stephen Still do, I'm not a bad person, and I'm sorry, but working for a charity and buying Fairtrade shit does not suddenly make you this great person, so don't do that thing, y'know? Mean, I care about child poverty, global warming, war . . . all the other stuff, seriously, I cry when I see kids dying on the news, I even signed up to one of those direct debits once (though that was partly 'cause the girl with the badge had a nice smile) but I did it. It's just that . . . the anger I feel when I see a malnourished child is nothing compared to the eye-popping rage when I stub my toe or lose my keys. I want to care more, I really do, I just . . . don't.

Jamie I look round, check if blondie's impressed, but she seems to have . . . left. Oh well, in for a penny. Here, take your stinking dog meat, I say, and throw the kebab at him. Bullseye! Dripping all down his fat fucking face. He's livid, screaming blue murder, but knows there's fuck-all he can do about it, the spineless prick. Come on, mate, says Terry, leave it, he ain't worth it. And he's right. He ain't.

Helen I reach the burnt oak, the one hit by lightning, and I lean against it, out of breath. Light's falling. Look down. Funny the things you see every day but never notice. All this clover. Beautiful really. I look across at the metal sheds and next to them the scorched earth, where they burnt all the animals. I feel the bark of the tree. Rough, like your hands. I saw you by this oak, the day you left. I was in the kitchen stripping spuds for the dinner you never ate. I waved, but you didn't wave back and I could've sworn you saw me. Why didn't you wave?

Jamie Bit of a faux-pas regards the set-to in the kebab shop. Alex is a quarter Turkish. Forgot about that detail. Suffice to say, he is not impressed. Try to explain it's the heat of the moment, you say things, but he's not happy, he's gone all moody on me. Fuck's sake, if I'd known it was that big a deal . . . He'll be all right once I buy him a drink.

Stephen I'm slightly shocked to discover Ken is still talking. He's having a bit of a sincere moment, I think he's telling me about his home life, and I know it's wrong but I find my eyes wandering to the sign on the wall and then – bang! . . . like a cartoon light-bulb I remember what's in my briefcase. I packed a little special something. And it all becomes clear what I must do. I need to save Ken. Save myself! I think you'll like this.

Jamie Bit peckish, actually. Maybe I shouldn't have thrown that kebab after all. There a chippie near here?

Stephen Ken, I say. Ken stops, halfway through a moving account of the pressures he faces at home. Ken. You do know that you can't carry on like this, don't you? Ken nods, he understands (possibly even a little overwhelmed by my empathy) and as I pop the first catch on my case,

I nod back, sympathetically. Ken, I say. What are the three F's?

Jamie Alex nips into the park for a slash behind the war memorial while Mickey stops by the cashpoint. Terry takes me aside. 'Ere mate, he says, take it easy, yeah? What you talking about I say, take it easy? Back in the . . . Y'know, he says, just . . . Ahhh, you seen how these cunts treat their women. Come here, think it's like it is back home, well it ain't. Yeah, I know, mate, he says, I'm just saying.

Helen Do you remember the day they told us? The vet had just checked our farm and we were given the all-clear. Not one of our animals was infected, not one. Then two days later they confirmed a case at Dawson's farm and we were classed as contiguous and that was that, it didn't matter that we were clean, we were 'contiguous'. I remember asking you what contiguous meant and you said it means next-door and I said, so why don't they just say next-door?

Jamie Look, he says, not being funny, Jamie, but this ain't to do with your sister, is it? No, it fuckin ain't I say, the fuck you go bringing that up for? I'm sorry, mate, shouldn't have mentioned it. No, you fuckin shouldn't, I say. You tryin to spoil my night or what? Just worried about you, he says. Well, fuckin don't be. Well, I am, he says, 'cause I fuckin love you. You dirty bent bastard I say – come here! An' I fuckin kiss him right on the lips. Oi lads, less of that, queer club's that way, says Alex, returning from the park, doing up his flies. Listen, Alex, I says, I'm sorry about all the bollocks, y'know, it's my fuckin mouth. You're a cunt, says Alex . . . Come on, give us a kiss, he says, I'm feeling left out. All right, I say, but no tongues.

Stephen Ken! The three F's! Ken hesitates, I pop the second catch. I feel your pain?

Jamie Come on, we going to this club or what? Better wait for Mickey, says Terry, he's still getting his money. Oi, Mickey you twat, how long's that queue?

Stephen Good, Ken. And why do I feel your pain? Because you have felt it too, he says, sounding brighter already. That's right I say – because I have felt your pain too. And I have found the solution, says Ken, really quite chipper now. That's right, I say, as I remove the grenade from my briefcase. I have found the solution. And this is it, I say, holding the grenade aloft, one finger in the pin. Ken? Everything all right? You look a bit peaky. Why don't you take the rest of the day off? I say. As I remove the pin.

Helen This'll make you laugh. About a week after you left, a letter arrived from the Ministry, addressed to you, granting our second movement licence, remember, so we could give the cattle more space to graze? Anyway, this letter arrives. So I pick up the phone, dial the hotline, and after an age, this young girl answers. Can I have your property reference number? she says. No, I say. Don't you have it? she sighs. Tell her I've got a problem. What's that? she says. Well, my husband applied for a movement licence and – I'm sorry she says, if you have any queries regarding a pending application – I stop her. No, you don't understand. You granted the licence. Then how can I help you? You can start by telling me how I can move cattle I haven't got. What do you mean? she says. Well, a month ago, you see, you slaughtered them all. Oh God, she says, there must have been a mix-up, the letters must have crossed. I'm so sorry for you and your husband, I'm so sorry, she says, I'm so so sorry (I think she's sorry, what do you think?). Oh, don't be sorry for him, I say. He had a heart attack last week. He's dead. The sun is setting. I stand on the blackened earth outside the cattle sheds, peering into the gloom. I walk in.

Jamie Punters rammed in like cattle, a shiny-shirted herd of bodies, the curve of arse, the tightness of tit, the bulge of bicep all defining their market value. Every one of us looking for love (or a quickie in a cubicle, beggars can't be choosers). One nation, under a groove, it's retro night! Blokes in fake afros, birds in short skirts, all evoking the spirit of the sixties. I love empowered women!

Helen Stale air hits the back of my throat like musk. With it come memories. I kneel by the spot where I found you. Right here. Lying on your side, body curled into a question mark. Something I need to ask you. First, I –

Jamie Right.

Helen I take off my jacket. Then jumper. My shirt, and then my bra. Pull off my boots, slide my jeans over my thighs, whup!

Jamie Blonde girl at the bar, tight white party dress, vacuum-packed in, face ain't up to much, but tits like . . . Morocco. Oh. And a boyfriend.

Helen Overbalance and land on my arse. Bollocks. Head's a little . . . temazepam, diazepam and booze, all kicking in.

Jamie Redhead, bit flat-chested, but I like freckles.

Helen I slide out of my jeans, not feeling quite so dignified now. Remove my underwear, unscrew the cap from the container and douse my clothes in the white spirit.

Jamie Darling, did it hurt? What, she says, when I fell from heaven?

Helen I spark the flame on your lighter and . . . woosh – watch my clothes burn. Like the pyres.

Jamie Brunette, smashing figure, one of them crop-tops you can see her belly-button.

Helen Led them in here. They thought they were here to be sheared. I lied to them. Lied to my babies.

Jamie Love it when you can see a girl's belly-button. Really sexy. 'Ere, darling, anyone ever told you you're incredibly beautiful?

Helen Run my hand over my scalp. Feels rough. Can hear their cries. Help me. Help me. But we just watched, didn't we, stood by? Hooves banging against the metal, feet stamping. Gunshots. (*Sharp intake of breath.*) I lift the container, close my eyes and pour the contents over my head, slowly, over my shoulders, covering my breasts, my stomach, my thighs. Inhale (God, that's strong). I hope no one mistakes this for a cry for help.

Jamie I said, has anyone ever told you you're incredibly beautiful? She says something back. What? I say. She repeats, but the music's too loud, I can't hear. I see! So I lean in, cupping my ear to those luscious lips of hers. You're going to have to speak up, love, I say to her, the music's too loud, I can't hear a word. Fuck off, she says, in a loud clear voice.

Stephen I'm sat in an expensive bar with uncomfortable chairs. You'd like it. Sat here, God knows how long, drinking God knows how much, mulling over my little grenade fantasy, imagining what it would have been like if I really did blow everyone up instead of just saying, 'Thanks, Ken, that's all for now.' I imagine the carnage. Malcolm from downstairs with his leg hanging off. Stephanie with her face all melted. And then I see you, Sarah, lying under some fallen masonry. And as I stoop down to help you, you look up at me so helpless as if to say, no, go ahead, please do, no no, no one's sat there, yeah, course –

Jamie My last fucking night on English soil, just want to get laid, that too much to ask? Bloody hell, I'm asking for a shag not a soul-mate.

Stephen Angela! Wow! That's an intense name, I say to the pretty girl who sat next to me. Apparently she's waiting for 'a friend'. We're just talking, there's no need to be jealous, besides, you're a married woman. Anyway, I think you'd like her, she's in new media, whatever that means. 'Angela, you're an angel!' I say, really turning on the charm now. Angela's doing that whole looking-around thing that girls do when they're trying not to seem too keen. Do you want to hear my theory? I say to her (real cool). What's that, then? she replies, equally cool. That we are each other's angels, I say. That sometimes, and we may not even know this, we can be demons and angels to each other. That things we do, that may mean nothing to us, they may be extraordinary acts of kindness to others. Like I might make a cup of tea for someone and it's just a cup of tea, but for that person, at that time, it's everything, you know? And Angela, I know this'll sound corny, but right now, you're an angel to me. And fuck me if Angela doesn't start to cry. And suddenly everything's all right, Sarah, and I, I can see that maybe I was a bit hung-up on you and maybe I was having trouble letting go, but now I can because you see, I thought you were my soul-mate, but I'm sorry but you're not. Because she is. Angela, I mean. And, if you'll excuse me a moment, I'm going to tell her . . . Angela –

Helen Do you remember all the theories, all the people who said it was foreign meat the disease came in with? But it wasn't. It was us, farmers cutting costs, feeding cattle their own shit. You've got to laugh, Tom, you really do. You really do.

Stephen No, I know we just met but, no wai-wai-wait, hear me out, Angela, 'cause I've got to say this and I'm worried that if I tell you this it might put you off me and we're getting on so well and no, no, let me say this, let me say this, 'cause it's important 'cause I don't want secrets between us, no lies, 'cause lies destroy people, and

35

this is what I need you to know . . . if you can bear with this, no just WAIT! Sorry, I didn't mean to raise my voice, I just have a lot of anger inside. That's what I'm trying to tell you, that sometimes . . . Sometimes I imagine what it would be like to kill someone, to fucking rip out their heart or set off a grenade or . . . y'know? Y'know that feeling? That feeling when you feel like you could just . . . kill, just to feel something . . . What do you mean, I'm scaring you? Hey, no, hey, no no no, don't be afraid, I'm not a violent person I'm just in a difficult place right now, no, Angela, wait – and as Angela gets up to leave, I reach out to grab her to stop her, to tell her she's making a big mistake, but as I stand the room starts to spin, the nausea comes and . . . everything goes black.

Helen Sometimes the thought of you overwhelms me. I'll pick up a book or find something that reminds me of you, like a jumper or something silly like that, and it's like I'm possessed by this desire to feel you, to hold you, to make love to you, but at night I reach out for you and you're not there, so I, I think of you while I . . . it's stupid, but I imagine you're there with me, next to me, inside me, I think of . . . us. And for a few moments I feel flooded with warmth like I've stepped into a warm bath and it's . . . but then it's like someone pulls the plug out and the water goes and I'm left naked in a room full of cold air and I just feel – (*as if comprehending the full weight of the word for the first time*) – bereft. Like I've lost an arm.

Jamie Terry with a short blonde, Alex's hand up the redhead's dress, my boner pounds against the inside of my trousers in time with the beat. Let me out, let me out, he says.

Helen You will never know what that's, what that's like, and I want you to know, I want you to, because I am angry with you, I'm angry. Because you didn't prepare me for this. You didn't let me know how lonely this is and . . . why should I have to feel all these things without you to feel them with?

Stephen Lying in an alleyway, head pounding like a trance beat. Dim recollection of two bouncers carrying me out the back way. I need to go home.

Jamie I'm bored this stupid place, music's gone shit, the birds are dogs and I want to go home and that's the fuckin final straw. That bird in the crop-top's dirty-dancing with some foreign cunt. In't that always the way? Hang on, I know him from somewhere?

Stephen On the Tube, Angel disappears through the window, should be heading the other way must've gone north by mistake. Guy opposite stares at me, disgusted. Glance down, realise there's vomit on my shirt and dread to think what that wet patch signifies. Any case, personal grooming's gone right out the window. 'S okay, pal. You can stare. Believe you me, I share your disgust. It's Friday night, a packed Tube, and the seat next to me's been empty the last two stops. It's official. I have become the scary bloke on late-night public transport.

Helen You told me you went to the doctor about the pains in your chest, that's what you said, you told me he said it was fine. But you never did because at the funeral I spoke to him and he told me you never went. You lied to me! You lied. I felt so stupid. Stupid.

Jamie Oh, you got to be joking. No, you are taking the piss, mate! What's he doing here? He shouldn't be here! He should be banged up, getting done up the arse with all the other perverts, not here, not fuckin dancing. Don't ask me how or why he got out, but I'm sure it's him, the one, the one who . . . I'm steaming. Check for the lads for back-up but can't see 'em. Imagine not telling us, not telling my sister. What if she was . . . if she was doing her shopping one day, if she was out doing her shopping for cornflakes and milk and that and she just bumped into him? If she turned a corner in Asda, turned left at the frozen peas, saw him standing there, bag of carrots, y'know, what then? As if I'm having that. Mate. You're a dead man. Put my hand on his shoulder, ready to leather the cunt, and as he turns to face me I look him in the eye, say –

Stephen Something deep inside wells up, hope to God it's not more vomit and I'm on my feet 'fore the part of my brain responsible for stopping me can stop me. I'm going to die. I'm going to die, and I'm actually saying this out loud. We're all going to die, mate, shouts some wag. No, I say. I'm really going to die. I've got cancer. Yeah.

Jamie Sorry, mate. Thought you was someone else.

Stephen That shut him up.

Helen The flame on the lighter has gone out. My head's spinning a little, feeling a bit sick actually, but I'm going to do this, I'm going to finish this properly, I'm coming to be with you, Tom, and you can't stop me. But before I do, I've got a question for you. And I want you to tell me the truth, I need you to answer me and I swear I'm not leaving till I get an answer. Why did you leave? 'Cause that day you went into the field, when I waved, and you were by the tree and it was through a window, and I don't know, but the way you looked at me . . . I'm just going to ask, Tom. Did you know? I mean, did you know you were going to die, 'cause the thought that occurs to me and I feel sick just thinking about it, but did you maybe not tell me you were going to die and did you keep working and did you make yourself ill because you couldn't bear to be around me, that you . . . that you made yourself die because you didn't love me any more? Because that's what I'm scared about, because I can't carry on without you, because there's nothing left and I need to know that you loved me because that's the only thing I have left to keep me going. Do you? Do you? Do you?

Jamie Couple of shorts steady my nerves but to be honest I'm almost blind now with the need to get my end away and the prospect of another night alone with my hand and a roll of tissue just don't seem inviting for my last night on home soil. Fuck it, had enough of this shit, I'm off home. But then. At that precise moment, through the thick mist of sweat and smoke . . . she appears. Face like an angel, body built for sin, showing what she's got and boy she's got it. On her own, lines of defence weakened, not too steady on her feet looks of things. My angel in Lycra. No messing, eggs in one basket, look her in the eye say – darling, did it hurt?

Helen You idiot. You bloody fucking fool.

Jamie Hands over her arse, music, music so loud her arse feels like heaven.

Helen I hate you so much.

Jamie I'm going away tomorrow, I say, I'm going to fight for my country I might not come back.

Helen I hate you.

Jamie She smiles and shoves her hand down my trousers.

Helen I hate you so much.

Jamie Before I know it, she's dragging me to the Ladies, practically batters the door down, she's a big girl.

Helen You stopped talking to me and I don't know why.

Jamie First cubicle, someone having a shit, second cubicle's free, no lock but we don't care. Knickers and pants down round the ankles, skins in my wallet but cock's so hard don't ahhhhh . . .

Helen You left before I had a chance to ask.

Jamie My cock's so big and shiny it's like a bus.

Helen You didn't give me a chance to ask.

Jamie I'm Red Rum winning the Grand National, I'm scoring from the spot to beat the Argies at football, going over the top to fight you fuckers, winning the war single-handed.

Helen You didn't give me a chance to say goodbye.

Jamie Think of that cunt, what he done to my sister his foreign fuckin hands all over her laughing to all his mates after he –

Helen Why won't you answer me?

Jamie Should've been you tarts like you deserve that, not her, not her –

Helen I want to hear your voice!

Jamie Ah you dirty slag on my big cock you make me do this, you make me you –

Helen I want you to come and get me!

Jamie Ohhfuckohfuckohfuck.

Helen Brain's going now. Right knee gives way and I stumble. Nearly fall, regain my balance.

Stephen Two months ago, routine check-up turns nasty. Cancer cells rampaging through me like a marauding army, it's a massacre in there, a full-on ethnic cleansing, women-and-children-shown-no-mercy deal. No hope. It's in my bones. Soon I die.

Helen Stare at the flames around my clothes and spark my lighter.

Stephen Just saying, I'm not asking for sympathy.

Helen There are figures dancing in the fire.

Stephen Okay, maybe a little. So I look round the carriage for something, anything, some sign of life, but they're all too scared, wish it wasn't happening, hoping to God their stop comes soon – heads bowed, eyes to the floor, a carriage full of penitents, hearts brimming with guilty secrets. Because now I'm not just some arsehole on the Tube. I've got a story to tell. There's a certain dignity only death can bestow. For the first time in my life, people are feeling my pain. And I love it. Then . . . This is not in the script . . . This woman . . . 'Bout the same age Mum would be actually . . . Beautiful grey hair spills round her collar . . . Eyes like . . . She hugs me. Doesn't say a word.

Helen I think of our wedding day, your eyes on me as I danced. A wind comes up, the flame on your lighter dies.

Stephen Just hugs me.

Helen I light the flame again and think about how you held my face as we kissed.

Stephen Rubs my back, front of everyone.

Helen Pushing open the door to our room.

Stephen Holds me like I'm all that matters in the world.

Helen Your hands tracing a line across my face.

Stephen Feel so ashamed fall to my knees sob like a child.

Helen Down my neck.

Stephen Not this, Sarah, anything but this.

Helen Along my shoulder.

Stephen I've been ambushed by kindness.

Helen I remember your body when you undressed for the first time. You look so beautiful, so funny! Your hands on my stomach, the backs of your fingers brush my hips. You run your nails over my thighs. I can feel your hair in my hands. The small of your back. Your eyes so –
Your smile so –
Your chest so –
Your breath so –
Your weight –
Your –
Your –
Your –
Your –

Sharp intakes of breath, intense, ecstatic, peaking, then gradually subsiding, until calm enough to speak.

Jamie You bitch.

Helen I'm in a bath with you. It's warm. You're soaping my back and your arms are around me. Sunlight streams in through the open windows. You lean past me, pull the plug out and the water pours down the drain. Shift forward, try and put it back in but you hold me back, won't let me. Water's going, I struggle and fight but you're too strong. I watch, helpless as the last of the water pours away. All gone. Cold now. And I'm alone.

Jamie It's raining gently out now, mates are gone, need a piss, knees are proper shot tell ya, barely walk.

Stephen Exit the Tube, stumble up into the night, it's cold. I know this place.

Jamie Chinese fella taps on the shoulder. Not here, not here, he says. Fuck's it to do with you where I piss? This my restaurant, he says.

Stephen Of course. Thoughts gather like dead leaves.

Jamie Look, mate, I say. Soz I'm pissing in your doorway, but you're closed and – but he won't take no for an answer.

Stephen There's the park we used to walk some Sundays. There are the swings where I pushed you.

Jamie Get your hands off me, get your hands – don't mean to hit him but I do, self-defence really, serves him right.

Stephen And here's the end of your road, where late one night, scarved and huddled against the February cold, I stopped and kissed your upturned face, ripe like an apple and told you I would never leave you, ever. And I wasn't lying.

Jamie I get my sons! I get my sons! he shouts. That's right, you do that, pal, you do that! You get your sons! Come on then, I scream through the window. Come on, you bastards, I'll have the lot of ya, you yellow cunts! Come on! . . . Next thing I know, three waiters come out beat the shit out o' me. Fair play, they could probably have done some proper damage, instead they let me escape across the park, shouting after me as I head towards the church on the far side.

Stephen I'm dying, Sarah. And I have to tell you this because I think when I do, it might make you realise something. You know, I just think it's, y'know, it was only when Mum died and you were so good with Dad, and y'know, it was awkward 'cause we were about to break up and I just think it's . . . I don't know, I don't know why I'm saying this, I think I'm just saying that if you were around and I know you're not, but I mean what were those fights we had about? What were they actually about? You know, I remember one time arguing with you about a tea bag! I think at the end we'd pick fights with each other just to feel alive. This'll make you laugh, well, maybe, I don't know, but sometimes I'd fantasise you'd died in a car accident or a plane crash or a terminal disease. I'd hold your hand, whispering I love you as you slipped away. And you had this speech where you told me one day I would find someone else and I said there would never be anyone else ever. And you die tragically and I grieve, noble and dignified, and your family clutch me to their bosom, and actually it's not really that funny at all, is it? Anyway, in the end your mother and father persuade me to see other people 'cause it's what you would have wanted . . . Here's your front door. I lift my hand to knock.

Jamie It's cold in here, dark, and strangely peaceful.

Stephen You know Dad always liked you, he . . . I don't . . . The truth is I, I got scared and I don't think I could handle that, y'know, that I felt so um . . . I think it scared me that I loved you so much and, y'know, I . . . so I just, I, I was looking for a way to end it and that's why I shagged that girl from . . . then confessed it all two days later. Truth is I didn't have the guts to dump you so instead I came over, presented you with this neat little grenade and said, here – you detonate it. And you did.

Jamie I've never been one for introspection but when you're actually confronted with Jesus on the cross, it really makes you think.

Stephen Want to know something else funny, not funny ha ha, more, y'know . . . I cried when I got my next phone bill. Every argument, every evasion broken down, logged and dated. No hours, forty-eight minutes, seven seconds. One hour, two minutes, fifty-one seconds. No hours, no minutes, three seconds (your flatmate picked up, heard my voice, hung up). And in case any doubt remained, Friends and Family was on hand to clear things up. That last month we were together, guess who topped my most dialled numbers list? Eleven hours, thirteen minutes, forty-four seconds. The itemisation of the end (four point two p and over). I mean that really is funny, isn't it? Y'know that I actually think this way? I mean, what a nutcase . . .! Look, like I said in the e-mail, I'm sorry I couldn't make it on Saturday although I didn't actually have another wedding to go to but maybe you guessed that. And I just wondered if maybe I . . . you know, and I'm sorry to spring this on you, but I just think if I tell you that I'm dying, you know, if you knew that, that, that you would, it would throw things into perspective and that you might realise how much we had, and I can change and, and I know you're married, but he's a wanker. And I'm not. And that's got to count for something. And before I know what I'm doing, I'm knocking on your front door. An upstairs light comes on. And this is it. I'm going to tell you that I'm dying and you're going to come back to me, except . . . I'm not and . . . you're not and, I mean I can't . . . I can't tell you that. Because it's not true. I'm not dying. Well. In the existential sense, but not in any immediate way. I made it up. Sorry, it seemed a good idea at the time. I just thought it might make you see me in a new light. That my shitty behaviour might somehow become . . . poignant.

Jamie First time for everything, I suppose. Like breaking into a church.

Stephen Actually I take back what I said earlier. I am a bad person. The hallway light comes on and I think of cigarettes and videos and walks in the park. The chain slides across and what the hell am I going to say? I had this big speech about new beginnings but I'm not sure it's really appropriate now. Well, I say speech, more a series of themes to improvise around, kind of like jazz but hopefully without the twat factor. Then suddenly, as the door swings open, a thought pops into my head. You moved in with him four months ago. You haven't lived here for ages. And I am confronted with a woman I have never seen before in my life. Hello.

Jamie 'Member the tricycle Mum got you when Dad left? 'Member that day, come home from school, Mum in tears, pissed on gin, you, 'member? 'Member what I said? I says I look after yer, Mum, Sis, I look after yer. I'm the man of the house now, I'll look after yer. Di'n't though, did I? Something else I fucked up innit? You fucking stupid fucking fucking nothing you cunt you. Hello? Someone there?

Helen You're not coming, are you?

Jamie 'S only the bloody vicar. Got to hand it to him, someone broke in my church late at night, first thing I'd suspect is satanists, keep well away.

Helen Are you listening? Is anyone? Are you there? Because if you are, please tell me now. Please. I don't know what I'm doing. I don't even know who I'm talking to . . . Please . . . But there's no one here, is there? Face facts, I'm just some mad woman in a field. I light the flame on your lighter a final time, hold it to my body and . . . a voice stops me. I turn. And it's you. Standing in the entrance to the shed, silhouetted against the evening sky, it's you. What are you doing here?

Jamie Which, under the circumstances seems a reasonable thing to ask. Best be straight with the padre, don't want to freak the poor bloke out.

Helen I was passing, you say. I saw you come out this way and . . . I just wanted to see if you were all right.

Jamie No need to be alarmed, Father, I'm not a satanist, just some pissed cunt broke in your church.

Helen You look so young. You're shaking. You look scared.

Jamie Why have you come here? says the padre. 'Cause I'm pissed, I say. That the only reason? he says. And I start to cry.

Helen Will you give me the lighter? you say. But I need it. You don't need to do this, you say. Don't I? No. Are you sure? You mean I don't need to do this? No, you say . . . Have you come to rescue me? I say, and I feel a familiar flush of warmth. Yes, you say. You look so beautiful, so young. Do I look beautiful? Yes, you say. Really? Yes, but can you give me the lighter? you say. Will everything be all right now? Yes, you say, I think so. Good. Good. And you're bathed in an orange halo of light and you look like an angel, like an angel come to rescue me and the look in your eyes . . . like a star exploding somewhere deep within you, creating new galaxies, each one filled with endless possibilities. I think of all the things we've done together. Will you look after me? I say. Yes, you say. Give me the lighter . . . Okay. And I do.

Jamie He don't say a word. Don't need to. Just sits there while I cry like I have never cried and pour my guts out how this man this animal took my baby sister's dignity from her, how he . . . how he –

Stephen The last Tube has gone and it's too cold to wait for a nightbus so I head back towards the river, planning to pick one up on the way.

Jamie Know she was going college, she was . . . didn't even use a skin, the cunt, three months she thought she might have AIDS. AIDS? Like fucking junkies and arse-bandits. If you could only see her, how it's changed her, y'know, she come top of her class English, she did this story, it was . . . she wa'n't a thick cunt . . . not like her brother . . . they're not like us, I say, these foreigners, they ain't civilised.

Stephen The girl who lives at your old place was fairly good about things, what with it being long past midnight and me being – let's face it – completely hammered. Though, I must admit, when I told her I was looking for my ex-girlfriend and her husband, she did get a bit unnecessary, but that's London for you.

Jamie I promised her, right, promised her, I told her, I said.

Stephen When did this city get so big? Every day it seems to have grown, as if it's being fattened for sacrifice. Sure it wasn't this big last time I looked. I swear, one of these days we'll wake up and the whole world'll be London.

Jamie Dad pissed off years ago and Mum's no use, she's never around neither and when she is she's –

Stephen All in all I'd say today has been unusual – oop. Whoa. Lost a bit of time there . . . Gray's Inn Road. Oh, and there's my bus. And a guy mooning his arse out the back window. Shit.

Jamie I'm . . . I'm going to fight in a war tomorrow, kill some of those bastards . . . fucking . . . might die, y'know. Boom! Bit scared actually.

Stephen A wave of tiredness threatens to sweep me off my feet but I head on, past St Paul's towards Bank, down King William Street past the great Monument where something or other happened a long time ago, and as I head up a side street towards the bridge, dawn appears over the horizon. I head south over the river. They say when a man is tired of London he's tired of life. Though in my experience he just moves to Brighton.

Jamie I, fuck, y'know, I . . . you know, the answer, I mean – you know 'bout these things, don't ya? Mean 'f I die I go to heaven, yeah? Will go to heaven, won't I?

Stephen I lean over the side of the bridge, gaze down into the darkness and the river lunges up at me, immovable and mysterious, like a great dark, mysterious thing. Sorry if I'm sounding pompous, but seeing as I'm about to kill myself you'll forgive me some poetic licence.

Jamie I mean, y'know?

Stephen Clamber up the shiny stone wall, face the rising sun, spread my arms and I'm ready. One last desperate leap into immortality. Goodbye, Sarah.

Jamie Feel bit funny actually.

Stephen I imagine you crying when you hear the news, almost want to phone Dad, tell him which picture of me to give to the papers (gap year, stood by an ancient ruin in Greece, enigmatic and dashing). Deep breath, bend my knees and –

Jamie You hold me? Not bent or nothing but –

Stephen Okay, I'm going to do it. I'm going to do it. I'm going to – actually it's a fuck of a long way down.

Jamie You please hold me, Father?

Stephen What if no one notices? What if I do this and no one notices, that would be really shit wouldn't it, if I made this grand gesture all for nothing? Second thoughts, I can't do this to Dad. Besides it must be bloody freezing in – whoa!

Jamie Thank you, Father. Feels nice calling you that. All right I call you that, yeah?

Stephen I try to keep my balance but I can feel myself going. Bollocks. What an embarrassing way to die. Hope I'm not remembered for being a fuckwit. I mean, look at Elvis – all that great music and he's still known for dying on the toilet in a big nappy. And I haven't done half as much as him.

Jamie Rest now. Close my eyes.

Stephen As I fall, I think of something you said to my dad after Mum died, how sometimes it's all we can do to keep going. That sometimes that's the bravest thing we can do, just to wake up and keep plodding on even when it hurts . . . impact.

Jamie Where am I? Who are you? Fuck me, it's an angel. I'm in heaven. No, says the angel. This isn't heaven, it's a church. And my name's WPC Khan. I think we need to get you a bed for the night. Turns out the padre did call the police after all.

Helen Ambulance'll be here soon. Keep talking, keep talking, you say, ambulance'll be here soon. Keep talking. What shall I talk about? Anything, you say, anything you like, just keep talking.

Jamie Has anyone ever told you you're incredibly –

Helen Why did you leave me? I say. Why did you leave? I'm not going to leave you? you say. I'm not going anywhere. But why did you leave? I say. I'm here now. I'm here now, you say. You should've told me things, you should've told me things, and yes I'm angry with you but . . . I forgive you, Tom, I say. I knew you'd come. I knew you'd come, Tom, in the end, I knew. Your eyes are filled with tears. It's not Tom, you say, it's Daniel.

Jamie In a van, drifting off to sleep. Out the window see the sun rising.

Helen I know, I say. Goodbye, Tom. And I lean in, kiss you on the mouth.

Jamie Your lucky night, says the lady copper. No space in the cells, we're taking you home – anyone we can call? Mum or dad or someone (that's a laugh)?

Helen In the distance, sirens getting closer.

Jamie My own private taxi! Weyyy! What a night, eh? Top one. You what? You want my phone number? What you want that for? Thought you was on duty, love?

Helen Hang on, you say, hang on.

Jamie Listen, about all that bollocks earlier, y'know, about being scared an' . . . that's just the booze talkin', y'know don't listen to – wo wo wo, that's my front door, just drop us here, Jeeves, the lady of the house will be out presently.

Helen And I will see you, Tom. I will see you soon. If only I can make it back. Not Tom, you say, Daniel. I know, I say. I know.

Jamie Hello, Sis, what you doing up?

Helen I think of Henry the lamb. Think of that Monument in London. Think of our wedding night. But that's all in the past now. All in the past, isn't it?

Jamie Sorry, babe, think I overdid it, I didn't mean to wake you up and that.

Helen So much left to do. So much to live for.

Jamie Weyyy! Two lovely ladies, one on each arm!

Helen Hang on in there, you say. Hang on in there. I will, I say. I will.

Jamie Sis, I want you to know I, I, I –

Helen I'll see you soon, Tom. But not just yet, okay? Not just yet.

Jamie Want to make you proud. Whoo, up the stairs!

Helen Everything will be okay now.

Jamie Going to fight tomorrow, fight for our country, Sis.

Helen Everything will be all right.

Jamie You tuck me in?

Helen Everything will be just fine.

Jamie Read me a story – only jokin', babe!

Helen I can feel it in my bones.

Jamie 'S okay, Sis, I'll look after yer. I'll look after yer.

Helen Brain feels funny, not sure where I am. Sirens. Sirens and voices.

Stephen Where am I?

Jamie Look after yer. Now on, I promise, yeah.

Helen I'll be seeing you soon.

Jamie Promise.

Stephen Where am I? This doesn't look like heaven?

Helen Just not yet.

Jamie Fucked up, di'n' I, yeah?

Helen Not quite yet.

Stephen If it is, someone should have a word with God about the decor. Ow, motherfucker –

Helen Feel so alive.

Jamie Nice when you stroke my head.

Stephen Head's like a . . . Oh God, I hope I'm not –

Helen Awake.

Stephen Hang on, looks like London. I'm lying on the pavement.

Helen Alive.

Jamie I miss him, Sis.

Stephen Must've fallen the wrong way. Or is that the right way?

Helen (*continues underneath until her next cue*) Awake . . . Alive . . . Awake . . .

Jamie I miss him, Sis. He's a cunt, but I miss him.

Stephen I touch my head and my hand is wet and sticky. Already I can feel a massive lump. Somebody up there must like me. I don't know whether to feel relieved or humiliated. Or both.

Jamie I know he's a cunt, but I miss him, y'know?

Stephen Try to stand, but ohhhhh . . . bad idea, bad idea.

Jamie Sorry, yeah?

Stephen Look at my hand, every crease, every fold, a landscape in miniature. A rivulet of blood winds down a valley into my palm. Lift my fingers to my tongue. Tastes good. My bum's cold.

Jamie So fucking sorry.

Stephen I think of you and all the things we'll never do.

Jamie Love you, yeah?

Stephen The thunderstorm we will never shelter from, laughing.

Jamie Love ya.

Stephen The beach we will never make love on. The crap films we will never watch together.

Jamie (*almost inaudible*) Love ya.

Stephen Sometimes it's all we can do to carry on.

Jamie improvises from his dialogue above, and Helen continues her chant, like a heartbeat, underneath Stephen, barely audible. Perhaps Jamie simply mouths the words.

A dog bounces past followed by two joggers on a lead who turn, disgusted and amused. And I think of that woman on the Tube. And I think of love. And as the first rays of the new day reach my face, a strange euphoria rises and from somewhere, maybe that woman, I find the strength to carry on. I clamber to my knees and shout at the joggers. Today will be so different, I cry. Today I will be somebody. Today my work will be respected, I shout to their dog. My work will be respected and my achievements acknowledged before multitudes. Today I will build an edifice that future generations shall admire, I say, to no one in particular. Today will be a good day. I can feel it in my bones . . . I never did call Dad.

Helen (*continuing*) . . . Alive . . . Awake . . . Alive . . .

The lights burn brightly now, increasing in intensity. Helen, Jamie and Stephen are caught in the light as if confronted with something awesome, something at once beautiful and terrifying and beyond comprehension.

Helen (*sharp intake of breath*)

And as the characters are enveloped in whiteout, there is silence and . . .

Blackout.